WHO RIGGED THE BIDS

Also by Vincent E. Green:

Corruption in the Twenty-First Century: Combating Unethical Practices in Government, Commerce, and Society

Government Ethics and Law Enforcement: Toward Global Guidelines (multiple authors)
Contributing Chapters:
"An Approach to Investigating Corruption in Government"
"The New York City Department of Investigation: Keeping an Eye out for Fraud in the Procurement of Goods and Services"
"American Institute of Certified Public Accountants: Government Brief"
Contributing Article:
"Vendor Integrity: Online Research"

VINCENT E. GREEN

Stepping up to
Combat Contract
Fraud in the City of
Brotherly Love

WHO RIGGED THE BIDS

TATE PUBLISHING
AND ENTERPRISES, LLC

Published by Tate Publishing & Enterprises, LLC
127 E. Trade Center Terrace | Mustang, Oklahoma 73064 USA
1.888.361.9473 | www.tatepublishing.com

Tate Publishing is committed to excellence in the publishing industry. The company reflects the philosophy established by the founders, based on Psalm 68:11,

"The Lord gave the word and great was the company of those who published it."

Cover design by Nino Carlo Suico
Interior design by Manolito Bastasa

Published in the United States of America

ISBN: 978-1-68254-832-5
1. Political Science / Corruption & Misconduct
2. Education / Educational Policy & Reform / Federal Legislation
16.03.01

The darkest places in hell are reserved for those who maintain their neutrality in times of moral crisis!

—Dante Alighieri

Contents

More to Come

I TRULY HOPE that you enjoy the first of this ten volume series on proven anti-corruption techniques.

I am confident that what you hold in your hands is powerful enough to be the opening salvo in your noble assault to vanquish corruption. I can say without fear of meaningful rebuttal that the addition of this volume to your arsenal of weaponry used to combat corruption will lead you to many victories in this crusade.

As you take aim on those who dare to challenge you in combating corruption, I would like to arm you with additional tactical artillery in the form of the following upcoming volumes:

Interview and Interrogation
Surveillance Operations
Procurement Fraud
Covert Operations

Tactical Communications
Case planning
Defensive Tactics
Integrity Investigations
Building a corruption fighting agency

Foreword

Everybody knows that the dice are loaded
Everybody rolls with their fingers crossed
Everybody knows that the war is over
Everybody knows the good guys lost
Everybody knows the fight was fixed
The poor stay poor, the rich get rich
That's how it goes, everybody knows

—Leonard Cohen, "Everybody Knows"

It's pretty easy to be cynical about public corruption. Abuse of power by political leaders and government employees goes back to the beginnings of recorded history, and even casual readers of the news will encounter too many stories of graft. Nevertheless, the book you are about to read is a powerful and effective antidote to feelings of cynicism and helplessness. Vinny Green, for whom I had the honor of working for seven years, is one of the leading contemporary voices advocating for a crusade against corruption, which he rightly sees as an insidious disease that erodes confidence in government and which has pernicious effects both seen and unseen, including increased disengagement from the democratic process and the loss of hope in a better future.

Vinny's remarkable and inspiring career has positioned him perfectly to be a preacher for fighting the good fight, as he has done for more than thirty years. In 1980, he began as an entry-level investigator with the New York City Transit Authority Bureau of Special Inspections.

He joined the New York City's Department of Investigation, one of the oldest law-enforcement agencies in the country, as a confidential investigator in 1981. Two years later, he created the first Bureau of Inspectional Integrity. It was a bureau charged with uncovering and terminating corruption schemes connected with the vast New York City residential-housing market, serving as a special deputy United States marshal in the process. Over the following three decades, he rose through the ranks to become deputy commissioner for administration and operations, the first-ever DOI entry-level investigator to achieve that senior position. In that capacity, Vinny had responsibility of overseeing anticorruption efforts for more than twenty municipal entities, as well as managing DOI's more than $20 million budget.

Under Vinny's leadership, DOI investigators ferreted out what was, at the time, the largest fraud scheme in the history of the city and recovered $20 million for the people of New York. The investigation resulted in the arrests and convictions of agency managers, supervisors, clerks, and members of the public who orchestrated and participated in the scheme to defraud the people of the City of New York.

Vinny created and directed the Law Enforcement Training Academy at DOI. In 2010, he was tapped to create the first-ever Department of Vendor Integrity and Investigations for the City University of New York (CUNY), focusing his efforts on safeguarding the multibillion dollar construction projects being taken on by CUNY.

His practical experience has benefited students at the College of New Rochelle's School of New Resources, the City University of New York's John Jay College of Criminal Justice, Wagner College, St. Francis College, and the University of Findlay.

Vinny's credentials qualified him to share his knowledge on an international stage, educating leaders and dignitaries of more than seventy-five countries, including the Republics of Georgia, Tanzania, and Liberia. In Haiti, he met with both the president and prime minister of that country to provide recommendations on establishing anti-corruption programs for their country.

Over thirty years of encountering abuses of power and greed have not turned Vinny into a cynic. As you will see in the following pages, derived from a series of lectures he gave to the Philadelphia Housing Authority's corruption fighting investigators, he remains a passionate and inspiring crusader with a powerful message—that corruption can be fought successfully and that there is no such thing as a bystander in the struggle.

—Leonard I. Picker
Special Counsel and Director of
Compliance & Investigations
New York City Tax Commission[1]

1 Affiliation is for identification purposes only; the views expressed herein are solely those of the author.

PREFACE

Without Wax

WHILE READING A book by Dan Brown, I came across the phrase "without wax." As an individual who has championed the cause of integrity for most of my life, even as a child, Dan's explanation of the phrase has stuck with me ever since. While an old wives' tale, the history of the expression without wax is still, in my view, a fearsome foundation on which to build a lesson of integrity.

Without wax has its roots in the Latin words *sin* (without) and *ceras* (wax). It has often been said (incorrectly) to be the origin of the English words *sincerity* and *sincerely*. It is doubtless that many of my readers have used the ending phrase "Sincerely yours" in closing out letters, professing the authenticity of the letter's content.

As explained by Mr. Brown, without wax was used when a sculpture had a flaw. Artists of the time would fill in the imperfection with colored wax to match the color of the sculpture. The wax was, in essence, hiding or covering up defects in artwork. It was said that when an artist presented a piece of work as high quality, it was said to be without wax. Many pieces even carried a stamp on them with the phrase without wax, giving the potential buyer the assurance that they were receiving a work of quality or integrity.

While I am not in a position to attest to the accuracy of the origins of the phrase, I believe that the seed of integrity planted by these simple words, without wax, has the potential to reap a bountiful harvest in the fertile fields of *honesty*, *character*, *accountability*, and *self-restraint*. With this in mind, I present this work to you, without wax.

What you are about to read is a follow-up of my recent work entitled *Corruption in the Twenty First Century: Combating Unethical Practices in Government, Commerce, and Society*.

What you hold in your hand or see on your screen right now focuses on a particular type of corruption known as bid-rigging. I am providing this information in the hopes of not just sharing what I have learned in more than three decades in my quest to bring corruption to its knees but also to put into action practical ways of detecting and combating this specific type of corruption.

In all of my teaching, training, and writing, I never miss an opportunity to make the statement that "nothing in life happens in a vacuum." Whether you intend it to or not, what you do, what you say, and what you believe in will have an impact outside of your personal space.

The fact that you exist has an impact on someone else's existence. This is not a difficult concept to grasp. It is straightforward; because you breathe, others have been changed. With that stated, I believe—in fact, I know—that it is my responsibility to ensure that my existence has meaning, as well as a positive impact on those whom I interact with in an effort to eradicate corruption.

I once again offer up a clarion-call and invite those courageous souls who have already taken, or will be taking, up the challenge to reduce corruption to its knees, to dip into the well that I am humbly digging with these words. Drink from my encounters, and begin to cultivate a crop of anticorruption victories.

It is my fervent prayer that these words are the equivalent of a seed, planted in expectation of garnering a strong crop of anticorruption warriors. With this seed, I take the next step in humanizing a new generation of combatants, with the intended goal to make them more knowledgeable, better trained, and endowed with a stronger sense of commitment than the current generation of corruption fighters. I strongly believe that the cause to eliminate corruption is a formidable undertaking, but one that can be achieved if those enlisting in the struggle pledge to the undertaking with an unyielding fortitude and grit to endure until the manifestation of the complete and total eradication of corruption and its hideous offspring.

The detection and deterrence of corruption among the ranks of public servants, contractors, and those receiving benefits from the government serves as a proclamation of the strong public policy of ensuring the integrity of government to the citizenry.

It has been my esteemed fortune to be a willing combatant, for more than thirty years, in the global effort to combat corruption and fraud.

It is with ineffable joy that I pen these words with the intent of preaching the gospel of integrity and necessity of high ethical standards. The absence of integrity, a wayward moral compass, and low ethical standards have become a parasitic coalition in muffling the voices of the victims of corruption. It is the commitment to oppose challengers and stand firmly in support of a corruption-free environment that is lacking in many instances and contributes to the continued existence of this pestilence.

The prophet Ezekiel wrote, "And I sought for a man among them that should make up the hedge, and stand in the gap before me for the land, that I should not destroy it: but I found none" (Ezek. 22:30).

We must draw a line in the sand and let it be known that the immovable, unshakable gap between integrity and corrupt practices has been reinforced in the form of those digesting these words. William Shakespeare wrote in *Julius Caesar*, Act III, Scene II, "The evil that men do lives after them; the good is oft interred with their bones."

I say that the good men and women of integrity can contribute to building nations of honor and high ethical standards upon the worthless carcasses of soulless men. We shall adorn the chest plates of righteousness and move from street to street, town to town, state to state, and nation to nation and vanquish the festering pustule known as corruption. I believe with all of my heart that this can and will come to pass.

Dante Alighieri's Depiction of the Nine Levels of Hell in *Inferno*

The Eighth Circle of Hell: Fraud

Introduction

Corruption is not an accident, it is an outcome

—Vinny Green

FOR MANY PEOPLE, frauds such as bid-rigging exist as a sound bite on the evening news, or at best, a brief conversation amongst friends and co-workers acknowledging its existence and the shame of it all, but most will take no action in response. The reality is that bid-rigging, like all forms of corruption, is more akin to a vampire bite, sucking the life's blood from a society, killing some and far too often converting others to its life-draining cause. Like the cowards that they are, those who engage in bid-rigging schemes operate in the dark and are no respecter of men. These soulless schemers prey upon the young and the old, the rich and the poor.

Honest contractors and agencies that authorize contracts are not the lone victims of these schemes. As we will be discussing at length in this particular publication, the people of Philadelphia are the true victims in these conspiracies. There is a human factor to these frauds that perpetrators rarely think about, which transcends the almighty dollar.

Race, culture, and ethnicity hold no barrier against this fraud. Bid-rigging and its deceitful siblings and dishonest offspring hold a universal passport into our lives, communities and culture. It has successfully slipped into all governments and societies. This includes the City of Brotherly Love.

Those of us who are not confronted with the realities of the fraud occurring in our everyday lives, fail to take the time to think about how a $45 million procurement fraud, which is just the cost of one of the many schemes uncovered in the Pennsylvania Turnpike construction project, impacts the everyday life of the citizens of the city of Philadelphia, state of Pennsylvania, the nation, and quite honestly, the world.

Corruption has had a worldwide impact on the human condition. It is the most successful and enduring serial killer known to humanity. It is an impact that far too many of us in well-developed nations are blind to. It is estimated that some 21,000 children die every day around the world as a result of causes related to corruption. That is equivalent to

- 1 child dying every 4 seconds
- 14 children dying every minute
- A 2011 Libya conflict-scale death toll every day
- A 2010 Haiti earthquake occurring every 10 days
- A 2004 Asian Tsunami occurring every 11 days
- Some 92 million children dying between 2000 and 2010[1]

The silent killers named lack of integrity, moral bankruptcy, and ethical ignorance manage to have their hand in the demise of nearly 7.6 million children each year; yet these agents barely earn even a headline in true political debate, much less sustain primetime media coverage.

What you are about to read will provide detailed insight on combating bid-rigging. These words are presented with a certain level of humility. They also come from someone who has investigated or managed thousands of corruption investigations over a span of more than thirty years and has an understanding of best practices to employ in combating corruption.

1 "Today, around 21,000 children died around the world," http://www.globalissues.org/article/715/today-21000-children-died-around-the-world (accessed June 28, 2014).

Government of the People, by the People, for the People, Shall Not Perish from the Earth

Establishing an organization of unquestionably integrity begins with an honest assessment of yourself.

—Vinny Green

A large percentage of corruption occurring within governments worldwide relates to the procurement of goods and services. Every day, billions of dollars in procurement transactions take place worldwide. It is unfortunate, but not every dollar ends up in the hands or accounts of the intended recipients. In a multitude of instances, these funds are redirected, embezzled, stolen, or just wasted.

Fraud in the area of construction is commonplace and seems to be endemic across Australia, Canada, India, the United Kingdom and the United States, according to a recent report from Grant Thornton. Construction fraud itself has amassed a global price tag of approximately $860 billion. It is projected that the annual fraud cost in construction will rise to $1.5 trillion by 2025.[1]

The greatest threat of fraud in many organizations comes from within. Far too often, it is given life through employees at all levels, including senior management.

Political figures can also facilitate procurement fraud. One of the most lucrative fraud schemes in the corruption world is that of bid-rigging. A successful bid-rigging scheme encompasses a myriad of different types of schemes that, if successful, can be a jumping off point for countless other types of fraud.

Governments worldwide need to acknowledge that it is time to retreat from the daily impotent lip service they give on the topic of corruption, fraud, waste, and abuse in society. Leaders must begin to devise concrete plans of action to take hold of this rabid tiger affecting society—not by the tail, to be dragged through the jungle, but around the throat, choking off the air that gives life to the schemes that stifle the growth and success of government programs designed to uplift and sustain the people.

---

1 "Construction Fraud Costs an Estimated $860 Billion" http://www.natlawreview.com/article/construction-fraud-costs-estimated-860-billion (accessed August 8, 2014).

It must be clearly understood that the primary function of government is to procure services for the people. Without procurement, there would be no hospitals, trains, planes, and automobiles.

Without a well-planned and well-executed procurement process, there would be no means to secure the goods and services required to educate the people, defend communities, build roads and bridges, and in the case of the Philadelphia Housing Authority (PHA), provide suitable and affordable housing for the people.

Simply put, without procurement, government would cease to exist. It is a monumental undertaking that all governments take on in support of the people, as well as the development and sustainability of a way of life. Unfortunately, with that endeavor also comes an effort by those who would undermine good government by attempting to achieve a personal benefit by corrupting the established governmental processes, not solely by outside forces, but sadly, also from within.

It takes a fighting force

To prevent this unethical and illegal behavior, governments have—or are in the process of creating—organizations with the primary function to identify and eliminate corruption, fraud, waste, and abuse. One such organization exists in the city of Philadelphia, the Philadelphia Housing Authority's Office of Audit and Compliance (OAC).

There is a simple but clear message conveyed by the existence of OAC. The message is that those exploring the possibility of engaging in corruption must recognize that the OAC is the manifestation of the PHA's clarion call that enough is enough! The line has been drawn by the leaders of OAC. Let it be known that ne'er-do-wells and lawbreakers cross that line at their own risk.

The PHA has the right to expect the untrammeled benefits of free and open competition, i.e., the best goods and services at the lowest prices. In PHA's attempt to achieve this objective, it often relies on a well-established competitive bidding process.

It is critical to understand that the competitive process only works when participants set prices honestly and independently. Conversely, when competitors collude to compromise competition, prices are inflated, and the PHA is harmed. If the PHA is harmed, then the people of Philadelphia are harmed even more.

On an annual basis, the PHA spends millions of dollars to push forward on achieving the goals that it has formulated to improve the lives of those residing in PHA developments. This is not just about the tangible accomplishments that come with repairing or upgrading apartments and the developments overall. It also includes educating the contracting force that has been given the privilege of working with the PHA to meet the needs of the people. Too often, these organizations are reluctant and sometimes unwilling to comply with the rules and regulations that come with being a part of the PHA program.

G-Square Consulting Services LLC has prepared this publication for the expressed benefit of the OAC investigative effort in combating bid-rigging. It gives notice to those who dare to try to compromise the government fisc that they are coming up against a formidable force. A force committed to standing in the gap between those unethical parasites that prey upon the good works of government and those relentless warriors resolved to work for the good of the people. That formidable force comes in the form of the members of the OAC. The OAC is committed to ensuring that no fiscal harm shall befall the PHA while it goes about its mission of providing affordable housing to the citizens of Philadelphia.

OAC standing in the gap

In the state of Pennsylvania, bid-rigging is a violation of the Anti–Bid Rigging Statute. It is also a violation of the United States federal law known as the Sherman Antitrust Act. Many countries have similar antitrust-type statutes in their law books. The fact that such laws exist worldwide speaks, unfortunately, to the fixed presence of corruption in our lives. The existence of such laws also tells us that societies are staunch believers that corruption can and will be corralled

Bid-rigging is a scheme that has the potential to generate significant harm to the PHA budget and to compromise the procurement process in ways that results in increased contract cost through larceny. It is an incestuous scheme, usually requiring close relationships among the members.

Because of its incestuous nature, it is difficult to gain the cooperation of bid-rigging participants and prove the crime. Collusion among competitors in a bid-rigging scheme is a violation of the United States federal mail and wire fraud statutes, false statements statute, and other federal felony statutes. While it is a certainty that the PHA has been a victim of bid-rigging schemes in the past, it is just as certain that a well-trained and staffed OAC will be a fighting force that brings bid-rigging to its knees.

A Serious Battle Fought by Serious People

The score only matters at the end of the game

—*Vinny Green*

THE OAC IS accountable to the PHA for examining allegations of corruption, fraud, conflicts of interest, and other criminal activity or unethical conduct committed by employees, residents, and contractors doing business with PHA.

Employees have a responsibility to the PHA and the citizens of Philadelphia to report to the OAC, without undue delay, any knowledge or reasonable suspicions or beliefs that corruption or acts of serious misconduct are taking place. This includes offers or inducements emanating from a contractor to engage in unlawful activities.

As part of the PHA contracting process, contractors must recognize that by submitting a bid or proposal to PHA, there is an understanding of a willingness to cooperate with OAC in its investigations. If a contractor knows or reasonably suspects that another contractor or PHA employee is involved in misconduct, the contractor has a duty to report this concern to the OAC without delay.

The bright light of integrity

Price-fixing, bid-rigging, and other forms of collusion are harmful, illegal, and are subject to criminal prosecution by local, state and federal prosecutors. The OAC must send a clear and unwavering message that it is ever vigilant in the watch for corruption, fraud, and failures of integrity. When this attitude exists throughout the Authority, most employees and contractors will remain honest and productive contributors to the procurement ambitions of the PHA.

While all of the successful prosecutions targeting bid-rigging, price fixing and other forms of collusion are not widely publicized, do not fall under the mistaken impression that prosecutors are not on a regular basis successfully prosecuting conspiracies negatively affecting the procurement process.

The success of these prosecutions stems from the hard work and determination of committed investigators, such as those who make up the OAC—committed combatants focused on preventing corruption and shining the optimistic light of integrity in the face of those deficient in honor and veracity.

Education is the foundation

Many of these prosecutions spawn from the information provided by alert and dedicated professionals connected to or within the procurement process. This reaffirms that the key to combating corruption is not just vigilance; it is also very much about OAC being a platform from which to educate.

This education process includes (1) educating those charged with procuring goods and service, (2) educating those individuals who are the end users of these goods and services, (3) educating those entities holding or competing for contracts for goods and services, and most importantly, (4) educating the people.

This education process absolutely must include the implementation of corruption-awareness lectures for employees, contractors, and tenants. A critical component of any anticorruption program requires an intense and sustained corruption awareness program, or CAP.

For centuries, corruption has been the elephant in the room that no one willingly acknowledges as a problem. It has been treated almost as if it was a necessary evil, with a need to exist in order to sustain society as we know it. This is, without question, not the case. A competent well thought-out CAP will let the people know that they are not only encouraged to acknowledge the elephant but also to participate in shining a bright and blinding light of integrity into its face.

A successful CAP necessitates knowledgeable individuals committed to the anticorruption campaign, making scheduled visits to governmental organizations, schools, businesses, and community groups and giving presentations trumpeting the negative impact that corruption has on the organization, the government, and society.

CAP must stress the importance of the people reporting knowledge or suspicion of corruption and misconduct directly to the OAC. There can be no debate or wavering in this commitment. Like water behind a dam, corruption can and will find the smallest crack and begin to leak into our communities.

CAP programs with companies being awarded a PHA contract should include suggestions for provisions to include in the company's code of conduct, with respect to *fair* competition and no bid-rigging, as follows:

The ABC Company is a staunch supporter of fair competition and the free-enterprise system. With this support comes an unwavering organizational policy that no employee, owner, principal, key person, consultant or agent of this organization will enter into arrangements that unlawfully restrict its ability to compete with other businesses or their ability to compete freely and honestly with the Company. The Company's owners, principals, key people, employees, consultants, and agents are prohibited from entering into any unlawful arrangements or understandings that affect the pricing practices of the Company or the terms upon which its services are contracted.

In addition, all purchases and subcontracts entered into by ABC or any of its subsidiaries will be made exclusively on the basis of price, quality, service, and ability to meet the Company's needs.

No ABC owner, principal, key person, employee, consultant, or agent may enter into or attempt to enter into any understanding or take part in any scheme or plot to rig bids or in any way unlawfully interfere with another company from fairly bidding on a contract. Nor may owners, principals, key person, employees, consultants, and agents of ABC, engage in restraint of trade or fair competition.

Company owners, principals, key person, employees, consultants, and other agents must make reasonable efforts to avoid conversations, both in public and in private, that might suggest any kind of collective action or common course of conduct among competing companies that is in restraint of trade or fair competition.

If an owner, principal, key person, employee, consultant, or agent of ABC has any concern that actions being contemplated on behalf of the organization may be or appear to be in violation of antitrust laws, he or she must present these concerns to management before moving forward with those actions.

The above is a foundation upon which to build a strong Code of Conduct in any organization.

Public corruption: a plague on our houses

Public corruption, born of greed and an unhealthy desire for power, has been a relentless assault on those intangibles that we hold dear in our society—honesty, character, accountability, and self-restraint.

Honesty: It has been said, "The saddest thing about betrayal is that it never comes from your enemy, it comes from your inner circle." It comes from those whom you allow to be a part of your team. This is not only an undeniably true statement; it is also the strategy upon which individuals seek to destroy nations and businesses. The beauty of honesty is that it encapsulates the essence of what an organization and staff should stand for.

With honesty, you get promise-keeping and trustworthiness. With honesty comes an unshakable position of knowing that loyalty is present. With honesty comes a vital ingredient in the recipe that allows an organization with an honest mission to mold and shape combatants infused with integrity.

Character: Abraham Lincoln once said, "Reputation is the shadow, character is the tree." Character is so much more than what we try to display for others to see; it is who we are, even when no one is watching. Good character is doing the right thing because it is right to do what is right. It is just that simple and at the same time so complicated for so many of us. It is character that in every case will determine how those around you will respond to situations and life's circumstances.

Without character, you have before you an individual of form without substance, willing to be shaped for personal gain with no regard for organizational well-being.

Accountability: In the words of Stephen Covey, "Accountability breeds responsibility." There appears to be a stunning lack of accountability in far too many organizations worldwide. This rebuffing of accountability by those in authority on multiple levels has translated into a failure to take responsibility, a failure to be honest about one's failings in this area, and a frightening lack of character where it is needed the most, which is in governmental organizations and business.

Self-Restraint: "Leadership consists not in degrees of technique, but in traits of character. Leadership requires moral rather than athletic or intellectual effort, and it imposes on both leader and follower alike the burdens of self-restraint" (Lewis H. Lapham). This is the lynchpin that holds integrity in place. It is in the beauty of self-restraint that you will find success.

These are the values that bind the leaders of society and the people together. These values cross class and socioeconomic lines. When the people perceive or actually know that their leaders are deficient in these values, the government loses legitimacy. In that environment, the seeds of alienation, apathy, and discord will take root—not like budding flowers, but like strangling weeds.

Unethical behavior, associated with any government, creates inefficiencies within its ranks, and corresponding inefficiencies within a nation's economy. When a government functions with bribery as its fuel, destabilization is eminent and barriers to fair trade are created. In the twenty-first century, the negative impact of this destabilization and these barriers are not confined within a government's jurisdiction; it seeps into the air like a harsh pollutant and passes on from nation to nation.

Corruption-fighting cannot be a haphazard, chaotic undertaking where anyone with a badge, automatically gets a seat at the table. Not every law enforcement agency is suited for taking on this cause. It requires a working knowledge of the areas of government compromised while at the same time possessing the skill set to conduct criminal investigations, systems reviews, and efficiency checks, as well as communication skills and, most vital, report-writing skills.

Corruption investigators are not made on an assembly line or rolled out of a training academy. A skilled artisan must mold them. Having an organization in place dedicated to this undertaking is a much better fit in this fight than to make corruption-fighting one of the many tasks that a law enforcement agency is empowered to take on. When it comes to the integrity of the PHA, OAC is that entity of enforcement, well suited to meet the challenge of combating corruption. OAC is the positive light of integrity within the PHA, formed to serve the people. It is the force empowered to hold back and, through its proficiency, divert the drowning waters of corruption.

Nothing new under the sun

Procurement fraud and bid-rigging are not new to PHA, the United States, or for that matter, a recent phenomena to the world at large. In fact, procurement fraud can be traced back to mankind's earliest history books and religious text. The story of Cain and Abel, as expressed in the Muslim, Christian, and Hebrew faiths, tells of a tragic situation where two brothers enter into different professions; in modern-day language, one was a farmer and the other a rancher. In short, their story is not only the first murder recorded by man; for some, it is the first known instance of competition and ultimately, corruption among contractors.

In brief, Cain slew his brother Abel, essentially over a dispute relating to the quality and acceptability of their products. When God asked Cain where his brother was, Cain's evasive response was, "Am I my brother's keeper?"

Thousands of years have passed since Cain slew his brother over a contract dispute, and man repeatedly asks this question when it comes to monitoring the activity of his "brothers." In the world of corruption and fraud investigations, what is essentially being asked by initiating the investigative process equals the question first asked by Cain, "Am I my brother's keeper?" The short and long answer to the question is an unquestionable yes!

It is all about leadership

Fighting corruption is very much an art form. It requires strategic thinking and very often a sense of risk-taking not found in every type of investigation. Operating in the world of white-collar crime requires a certain level of competence in bluffing, politicking, and maneuvering in and out of the world of the white-collar criminal that is not called for in several other areas of crime fighting.

In this world, an effective corruption investigator needs to be armed with a formidable arsenal of weaponry. I am not talking about guns, handcuffs, or impact weapons. I am talking about the most powerful weapon an investigator has at his disposal. Some call it the gift of gab; I call it shooting from the *lip*, the all-powerful ability to communicate. This is a defensive, as well as an offensive, weapon that will be of great assistance; it has the ability to extricate an investigator out of more jams than any physical weapon ever devised by man.

The first strategic move in curbing corruption is to take the tactical position of stepping out in faith and establishing a leadership role in the fight. This means communicating with the people, both good and bad.

In 1890, Ohio United States Senator John Sherman took such a step by engaging congress to work with him to enact the Sherman Antitrust Act. It was a groundbreaking piece of legislation intended to prohibit anticompetitive practices by organizations. The act prohibits any agreement among competitors to fix prices, rig bids, or engage in other anticompetitive activities.

Violation of the Sherman Act is a felony. If the violation was committed before June 22, 2004, it is punishable by a fine of up to $10 million for corporations and a fine of up to $350,000 or three years imprisonment (or both) for individuals. If the offense was committed on or after June 22, 2004, the maximum Sherman Act fine is $100 million for corporations and $1 million for individuals, and the maximum prison sentence is 10 years.[1]

A Sherman Act conviction can result in an individual or corporation being court-ordered to make restitution to the victims of the misdeed. Those victims may also seek treble damages, which is civil recovery of up to three times the amount of damages suffered.

Taking shape

Most Sherman Act prosecutions, or its state or local equivalents, involve price fixing, Bid-rigging, or market

1 "Bribery in the Construction Industry: Part II—Bid rigging," http://enewsletters.constructionexec.com/managingyourbusiness/2013/01/bribery-in-the-construction-industry-part-ii-bidrigging/ (accessed June 28, 2014).

division or allocation schemes. To prove the existence of any of these schemes, it is not necessary that the conspirators enter into a formal written agreement. In fact, in most instances of bid-rigging the participants enter into clandestine verbal agreements in formulating the scheme.

Bid-rigging, price fixing, and similar criminal activity can be presented in court proceedings through the testimony of a participant, which would be received as direct evidence, or by a strong paper case supported by such documents as a bid-rigging checklist or bid-rigging matrix in order to build a strong circumstantial case.

Price-fixing

Any plan to fix prices violates the Sherman Act as well as laws enacted in many other jurisdictions. Price-fixing, by definition, is an agreement among conspirators to control the price at which commodities or services are sold. The success of price-fixing schemes does not require that all competitors participate in the scheme.

The Anatomy of Bid-Rigging

. . . when a person voluntarily accepts a position of public trust, he takes on new obligations. If he does not want to live up to them, he is free to decline the job. Not only is this a fair demand, but granting authority without expecting public servants to live up to it would be unfair to everyone they are expected to serve. Raise the salaries if jobs merit higher pay, but not in expectation of buying integrity. Nobody sells that. People who have it give it for free.

—Edwin J. Delattre

In the state of Pennsylvania, the definition of bid-rigging is the concerted activity of two or more persons to determine in advance the winning bidder of a contract let or to be let for competitive bidding by a government agency. The term includes, but is not limited to, any one or more of the following:

(1) Agreeing to sell items or services at the same price
(2) Agreeing to submit identical bids
(3) Agreeing to rotate bids
(4) Agreeing to share profits with a contractor who does not submit the low bid
(5) Agreeing to submit prearranged bids, agreed-upon higher or lower bids, or other complementary bids
(6) Agreeing to set up territories to restrict competition
(7) Agreeing not to submit bids[1]

The existence of a bid-rigging scheme in the PHA procurement process has the potential to do significant harm to the contracting process. A successful bid-rigging scheme can increase project cost and compromise the procurement process. Corrupt individuals usually work independent of government officials when attempting to execute bid-rigging schemes. However, in these schemes, there is a heavy reliance on the cooperation of conspirators to do their part in controlling which conspiring contractor will be awarded the contract.

Bid-rigging is a complicated scheme to prove. It requires detailed document review of bidding histories, bid tabulation sheets, individual bid submissions over a period of

1 Anti-Bid Rigging Act, Title 62, Commonwealth Procurement Code Pa.C.S. 4501 et seq

time, and in most cases, the cooperation of a participating conspirator. It is not just a matter of fraud. It is equivalent to the participants stealing the contract. As such, it is my opinion—based on the harm that I have seen because of bid-rigging over my career—that participants in these schemes should be charged with larceny corresponding to the dollar value of the contracts and not just the act of rigging the bid. Bid-rigging harms the PHA, honest contractors attempting to compete fairly, and it harms the tenants of PHA developments.

Where does it begin?

Many investigators and prosecutors are under the mistaken impression that bid-rigging schemes are initiated during the course of the actual bidding process. The reality is that very often these schemes begin to take shape well before then. Many begin with the formation of the idea of procuring a certain commodity. Often the idea originates with a contractor who wants a government contract and uses a procurement official as the avenue to provide the contract.

There is not always a government need for the services or items procured. Nevertheless, what does exist is the greed of the contractor and procurement official. When a coconspirator includes a procurement official, there exist an easy way to rig the bid. The rigging process can begin with the early release of information on the specifications and cost estimates to preferred contractors.

Another common component of rigging bids in the early stages of the process is where corrupt procurement officials allow consultants or others to assist in the drafting of specifications of a contract and then allow that same contractor to compete in the bidding process for the procurement.

The inherent conflict in condoning this process is that these contractors not only have advance notice of the procurement, they also have very specific information about the specification content. In many instances, that specification will contain requirements that only the contractor with advance knowledge can meet.

Incumbency, the unwritten award

These bid-rigging schemes often begin as a simple instance of the conspiring contractor being the incumbent on an upcoming bid solicitation. It is important to understand that in the specification-writing stage of the procurement process, incumbency, while not a necessary or mandatory component of bid rigging, can in fact be a leading contributor to the bid-rigging process. In a number of cases when the PHA is about to rebid a contract, the incumbent contractor, meaning the contractor that has the current contract has a significant advantage over potential new bidders who have not been involved in similar contracts with the PHA in the past.

This advantage does not initially exist because of any corrupt intent. It exists because the incumbent contractor has had the opportunity to work with the PHA and its procurement officials and end users in the normal course of day-to-day business. In so doing, the incumbent has established a much better understanding of the PHA's needs than he had prior to award of the contract.

In many instances, the contractor begins to understand the agency needs better than the procurement official. This superior understanding comes about because the procurement official, in most instances, is managing several contracts. However, the incumbent, who is only focusing on his contract, develops a far greater understanding of what is needed and not needed in any new specification being written and is now able to prepare his new bid from that unique perspective.

In many cases, the procurement officer has established a comfort level with the contractor and his employees, creating a conscious or subconscious bias. While this is a byproduct of incumbency and largely human nature, it also gives the incumbent an advantage when it is time to rebid the contract. In addition, it can and has led to the establishment of corrupt relationships. This is why it is essential that procurement officers and investigators alike take the specification-writing stage seriously and not treat it like a cookie-cutter exercise.

In taking it a step further, there are also instances where procurement officers will recognize the unique perspective that the incumbent contractor enjoys and makes the conscious decision to consult the incumbent contractor when preparing specifications for the new contract. While this might make the procurement officer's job easier, it gives an additional unfair advantage to the incumbent contractor. The practice ultimately creates a disadvantage for competing contractors and has the potential to cause fiscal harm to the PHA.

Specifications Must Be about Agency Need, Not Contractor Greed

Whatsoever a man soweth, that shall he also reap.

—Galatians 6:7

THE PREPARATION OF contract specifications is the step in the procurement process where the contracting entity sets out what specific goods or services are needed in quantity and quality. The specification will alert potential bidders as to what the PHA wants and gives the procurement official the basis for evaluating and accepting bids. A well-written specification will clearly present what the PHA needs and expects from a contractor.

This is also the point in the procurement process where collusion between the procurement official and contractor can begin to take root. A vaguely written specification might not be by accident but done intentionally to provide the contractor with a means to claim entitlement to additional money to supply the PHA with what it originally intended to receive. This usually comes in the form of a change order.[1] Alternatively, a specification written too narrowly can result in a product that can be supplied by only one contractor; this could result in the false justification of a sole-source procurement[2] or set the stage to rig the bid.

There are instances where specifications are written in such a way as to favor the incumbent contractor participating in a bid-rigging scheme to the exclusion of other potential bidders. With this in mind, investigators should begin bid-rigging investigations at the specification-writing stage, as opposed to the award stage of the process.

If a corrupt procurement official or contractor can control the specification-writing stage of the bidding process, then they have access to an almost endless stream of the people's money. It is here where OAC must take a firm stand in the gap between integrity and corruption and

---

1 A change order is a charge for work not included in a contract's scope of work. Contract terms and contract law, as well as various laws, which vary by jurisdiction, for publicly funded projects, govern change order procedures and requirements. Fraud in this area is not uncommon.

2 Sole source is a process where the required goods or services are available from only one source. The agency seeking to enter into the contract must give public notice of intent to enter into negotiations with the sole source provider.

remain resolute like a dam holding back the polluted and destructive flood that corruption can be.

Building an Impenetrable Dam

A Philadelphia fencing contractor who was confident that he could successfully breach the dam of integrity and pull off a successful bid-rigging scheme found himself and his company amidst a flood of charges by federal prosecutors alleging multiple acts of rigging bids for Philadelphia contracts valued at more than $750,000 over a period of more than two years.

The principal of the company was sentenced to 5 months of house detention, ordered to pay a $25,000 fine and serve 5 years of probation. The business was fined $60,000 and ordered to pay $59,000 in restitution to the people of Philadelphia.[3]

During the sentencing portion on the case, the federal judge questioned why city officials had not monitored the contracts more closely. Corruption fighters face this ques-

3 "Judge: Bid Rigger Gets Home Detention Donald Mohl Rigged Bids on City Contracts worth $750,000," http://articles.philly.com/1994-06-23/news/25834440_1_bid rigging-home-detention-restitution (accessed July 1, 2014).

tion on a daily basis. Corruption-fighting is a profession where detractors—and sometimes, even supporters—will take every opportunity available to criticize the work of a corruption investigator.

It has always amazed me how resistant judges have been over the years at meeting out the appropriate justice for those who orchestrate and execute bid-rigging schemes and other forms of corruption. When I was in college, I worked as a store detective in a large department store. The shoplifters that I apprehended received much harsher penalties for attempting to steal a $300 stereo than the white-collar criminal who steals millions of dollars from the people. There seems to be a horrible disconnect between recognition by those who meet out justice for those engaging in corruption and an understanding of those same individuals of the ineffable damage that corruption truly perpetrates upon society.

There must be unity and a shared understanding of the mission between the corruption-fighting agency, the prosecutor's office, and the judge or arbitrator dispensing justice. Prosecutors and judges who do not have to face the short- and long-range effects of white-collar crime do not always see it as serious as some of the other crimes they deal with on a regular basis and not always deserving of the punishment allotted in the law. Viewing corruption through rose-colored glasses must end if this battle is to be won.

Simply put, the fight against corruption can be a difficult one. When corruption is uncovered, those in authority and those on the front lines of the fight are criticized for allowing it to take place, condoning, or even supporting its existence. When corruption remains undetected, those same individuals are criticized for not doing enough to address the problem, and yet the punishment in far too many cases remains a slap on the wrist.

A corruption investigator cannot be swayed by any of this. Politics and the party line can never be a part of the corruption investigator's creed. Corruption fighters are accountable to the people and must remain steadfast, immovable, determined, and ever vigilant in the quest for the truth and the fostering of a corruption-free environment. No matter how well a corruption fighter performs the mission, there will always be those who will challenge the outcome. Do not be disheartened by this; it comes with the profession.

Chose a Category—Any Category!

The challenge is to be a light,
not a judge, to be a model not a critic.

—Stephen Covey

Bid-rigging conspiracies can fall into one or more of the following categories:

Complementary bidding. Complementary bidding is a part of most bid-rigging schemes. It is also known as cover, courtesy, token, or symbolic bids. These bids are submitted above the price bid by the collusively predetermined low bidder. Oftentimes, complementary bids will include conditions that the submitting company knows will be unacceptable to an organization such as the PHA, resulting in the bidder being found nonresponsive. With these types of bids, it will be found that companies colluding in the scheme will consistently submit bids but rarely win. The purpose of complementary bidding is to paint a misleading picture that competition is alive and well when in fact, it has been placed in a coma.

Market allocation or market division. This scheme occurs when competitors remove competition from the process by agreeing to divide markets among themselves. This is done by establishing an agreement whereby, in place of competition, the participants allocate markets by predetermining which company will be assigned a customer or geographical area in which to operate. The success of market allocation, as well as some other types of bid-rigging schemes, relies on the participants' willingness to submit complementary bids to give the false impression that competition exists. Market allocation is illegal and violates the Sherman Act because it stifles competition.

Bid suppression. In bid-suppression schemes, one or more of the competitors expected to bid agrees among the conspirators not to bid so that the contractor chosen by the conspirators will be able to submit the winning bid and do so at a higher price. By keeping potential low bidders out of the contracting process, other companies involved in the scheme can submit inflated bids without fear of losing.

Bid rotation. Bid rotation conspiracies are similar to market allocation in that participants conspire to ensure that they each receive a piece of the corrupted procurement pie. However, in bid rotation, companies that conspire take turns winning the available contracts. It does not require an allocation of the market. It only requires that participants be patient and wait their turn. Beyond patience, the success of this scheme requires the submission of complementary bids by the participants not scheduled to win the bid.

Subcontracting. This method to rig the bids is common and usually happens in conjunction with complementary bidding. It occurs when contractors agree not to submit bids or, preferably, to submit complementary bids with the understanding that parts of the contract or some other benefit to be realized later will be subcontracted to the scheme's participants that did not win the bid. This can be in the form of providing materials or equipment on the project. Frequently, competitors who agree not to bid or to submit a losing bid will, in exchange, receive subcontracts or supply contracts in return for refraining from submitting a serious bid.

In almost all cases, winning bidders will need to obtain supplies to complete the project. If the company providing supplies for the project is a scheme participant, that company can play a major role in determining the outcome of the bid by quoting high prices for supplies to bid participants that are not members of the bid-rigging scheme. It is very important to make an effort at determining the degree of influence that suppliers have on a particular contract. Having a supplier as part of the bid-rigging scheme can ensure the success of the scheme.

There is no honor among thieves

In Shakespeare's *Henry the IV*, Part I, Falstaff proclaims that there is no honor among thieves. As the following cases will confirm, this sentiment applies wholeheartedly to corruption and other white-collar crimes. Most individuals involved in these schemes do not see themselves as criminals and feel that their allegiances are to themselves and in some cases to their families. The idea of an arrest and sentence to a term in prison is an insult to them.

On the other hand, most career criminals see being arrested as an occupational hazard and something that will befall them at some point in their felonious career. White-collar criminals almost never entertain the idea that their immoral behavior will place them in a cell next to a career criminal. When this possibility becomes a reality, there are few instances where an investigator skilled in interview and interrogation techniques will find it difficult to gain the cooperation of a scheme participant where significant evidence is presented.

Corruption, for the most part, is a team sport. There will be few matters investigated where the target acts entirely alone. In many investigations, it will be found that corruption is part of a scheme involving several people on different levels in the chain of command and varying levels of influence.

In these investigations, it will be found that it is the low-level person or an individual with the least amount of influence in the scheme who is the most exposed when it comes to detecting the corruption and obtaining reliable evidence. When enough evidence is amassed to sustain a criminal or disciplinary charge against the low-level person, it is then time to focus efforts on what is known as vertical corruption, the concept of the "little fish catching the big fish." In this tactic, an investigator will gain the cooperation of the low-level person in an effort to obtain evidence against those higher up in a corruption scheme or outside of the organizational structure.

Bid-Rigging at the PHA

That which does not kill you makes you stronger.

—Friedrich Nietzsche

There has been a host of bid-rigging variations perpetrated against governmental entities worldwide. As the following cases make plain, PHA has not been spared in this arena.

PHA case studies

A federal investigation uncovered evidence that a South Philadelphia plumbing contractor had engaged in a bribery and bid-rigging scheme intended to defraud the PHA. At the conclusion of the investigation, the contractor pleaded guilty to paying $3,200 in bribes to two Philadelphia Housing Authority officials to help get plumbing and heating contracts with the PHA. The criminal charges allege that the scheme was the path used to allow the plumber to obtain 151 PHA contracts totaling $388,115.[1]

Investigators conducting inquiries into allegations of corruption should always be sensitive to the fact that corruption schemes are not solo endeavors. Obtaining evidence on one individual does not mean that the scheme is dead or that all participants have been captured. A critical step in the investigative process is to look for an opportunity to obtain the cooperation of a subject or witness in an investigation. During the course of this investigation, investigators and prosecutors had this in mind, and they employed vertical corruption techniques to gain the cooperation of the contractor.

The contractor agreed to cooperate in the investigation and pleaded guilty to one count of bribery and one count of mail fraud. The contractor's agreement included him testifying against other scheme participants. This testimony was one of the main reasons that several other PHA employees pleaded guilty rather than go to trial. In addition to cooperating with federal prosecutors, the contractor agreed to

---

1 "2 Ex-pha Officials Accused Of Extortion They Took $27,000 For Inspections," http://articles.philly.com/1995-03-31/news/25699813_1_pha-inspections-extortion (accessed June 30, 2014).

make restitution of $57,000 to the Department of Housing and Urban Development and $38,000 to the PHA.[2]

The assistant United States attorney prosecuting the case recommended leniency to the judge overseeing the case because the contractor cooperated in the investigation. The contractor's cooperation earned him a letter to the judge from the prosecutor known as a 5K letter.

When the defendant in a federal case provides substantial cooperation in a case against other participants involved in the case or of interest to the government, the prosecutor can draft a letter to the sentencing judge detailing that cooperation and request a downward departure in the sentencing guidelines because of the defendant's useful cooperation. This is pursuant to section 5K1.1 of the United States Sentencing Guidelines. The letter is known as a 5K letter. While the judge is not required to reduce the sentence, he will consider the request and make a determination depending on his view of the nature and the value of the defendant's cooperation, along with the severity of the crime committed.

---

2 "Contractor Gets Probation for PHA Bribes Gerald Dicicco Had Faced 18 Months in Prison," http://articles.philly.com/1995-09-08/news/25716320_1_pha-bribes-count-of-mail-fraud (accessed June 28, 2014).

The United States district judge assigned to the case sentenced the contractor to 4 years of probation, a $25,000 fine, and 200 hours of community service.[3] The judge agreed to probation instead of a prison term after receiving the 5K letter from the prosecutor.

Nothing in life happens in a vacuum; corruption is no exception to this theory. Corruption cannot exist without human interaction. Its very survival requires a series of relationships. These relationships must exist in order to place schemes in motion. This means that whenever a corrupt individual is taken into custody, he or she will always have someone to give up as part of a cooperation agreement.

Never bypass an opportunity to flip an individual involved in a scheme. This practice should be a foundational piece of any corruption-fighting program. As an investigator, you must never make the mistake of thinking that an individual that you have built a successful corruption case against is the only player at the table. That is almost never the case. There is always another layer to the scheme or a completely different scheme in play that the individual can

---

[3] "Contractor Gets Probation for PHA Bribes Gerald Dicicco Had Faced 18 Months in Prison," http://articles.philly.com/1995-09-08/news/25716320_1_pha-bribes-count-of-mail-fraud (accessed June 30, 2014).

provide information about that will take the investigation to the next level of corruption.

The charges against the contractor involved in this scheme included the payment of $2,900 in cash bribes to the former director of maintenance for PHA and $300 to an accounts-payable supervisor. The director pleaded guilty to extorting more than $300,000 from various contractors. He paid back $225,000 of the bribes he received by cashing in savings bonds and emptying a safety deposit box where he kept some of the money.[4]

The bribes were paid by four contractors in exchange for rigging bids so that they would be awarded contracts at PHA as part of ongoing bid-rigging schemes. The judge sentenced the former director to serve twenty months in federal prison.[5] The accounts payable supervisor pleaded guilty but died before sentencing.

The contractors in this case were also charged with rigging bids on the contracts. Through a combination of complementary bidding and other forms of bid-rigging, they

---

4 "Ex-PHA Maintenance Chief Admits extorting $323,925," http://articles.philly.com/1993-06-22/news/25972010_1_pha-contractors-scheme (accessed June 30, 2014).

5 "Contractor Gets Probation for PHA Bribes Gerald Dicicco Had Faced 18 Months in Prison" http://articles.philly.com/1995-09-08/news/25716320_1_pha-bribes-count-of-mail-fraud (accessed June 28, 2014).

determined in advance which contractors would win each contract. Two of the four companies existed only on paper. Their paper existence gave the illusion that competition was alive and well in the process.

The PHA head of maintenance provided the contractors with PHA's internal pricing information so that the contractors would know how much PHA was willing to pay for their services. With this information, the contractors were able to inflate their bids without fear of detection.

The maintenance director also involved members of his staff in the scheme. He directed the contractors to "take care of the girls." With that direction, the contractors began making payments to two clerks who prepared bid documents and to the accounts-payable supervisor. The clerks each received $44,000, and the accounts-payable supervisor received $10,770.[6]

In addition to the cases above, three other individuals involved in bid-rigging and bribery schemes at PHA pleaded guilty to their offenses and were sentenced to house arrest and probation and ordered to make restitution.

6 Ibid.

One contractor was given 3 years of probation, order to perform 300 hours of community service and was given a $20,000 fine. He was also ordered to repay $86,800[7].

A PHA maintenance mechanic was sentenced to 4 months of house arrest, 2 years of probation, and a $1,000 fine. He was ordered to repay $4,000 in bribes he took during the life of the scheme.[8]

Another contractor received 2 years of probation and a $7,500 fine. He was ordered to repay $6,320 to PHA.[9]

Excuses are the tools of losers in life

In yet another case, a PHA manager pleaded guilty to her involvement in a scheme netting $25,000 in kickbacks for her from two contractors in exchange for their doing business with PHA. The manager was in charge of awarding small contracts for the PHA. She pleaded guilty to three counts of a twenty-two–count indictment against her, and after investigators employed vertical corruption

7 "4 Sentenced In Pha Bid, Payoff Scam All Got House Arrest Or probation, fines and restitution Ordered" http://articles.philly.com/1993-09-30/news/25986508_1_house-arrest-pha-housing-agency (accessed June 28, 2014).

8 Ibid.

9 Ibid.

tactics, she agreed to provide evidence against her co-conspirators.[10] At sentencing, she offered as an excuse for her behavior that the PHA culture of corruption beguiled her into criminal conduct.

Let us be clear about something—excuses are not reasons. In the world of corruption, excuses hold no value or any justification for engaging in misconduct. When it comes to engaging in corruption, excuses are lapses in character and integrity, not a justification to engage in criminal activity. If anything, this individual surrendered to Donald Cressey's hypothesis known as the Fraud Triangle, made up of *pressure*, *opportunity*, and *rationalization*.

In terms of pressure, many people who engage in corrupt behavior do so because of peer pressure, financial pressure, career pressure, and a host of other types of pressure that can enter into an individual's life and influence them into engaging in corruption. However, no matter what the pressure may be that manifest into an individual's life, the corrupt behavior is a choice—it is not a requirement. It is an excuse; it is not a reason.

10 "Ex-PHA manager pleads guilty to extortion," *Philly.com*, http://articles.philly.com/2011-05-05/news/29512993_1_kerri-bizzell-pha-extortion (accessed June 28, 2014).

With respect to opportunity, it is the most critical force in the fraud triangle. While pressure of some sort is an ever-present constant in the decision to engage in corruption, that decision cannot be implemented unless an opportunity exists for an individual to engage in the corruption. This can happen in many ways. Some of the common causes are poor supervision, lax controls, failure to implement a separation of duties, failure to implement a staff rotation policy, and the granting of too much trust or authority to an individual.

Individuals who engage in corruption will always seek to rationalize their behavior with excuses that the business owes them something or that they have been mistreated in some way. The excuses are endless, but they are just that—excuses, built on a foundation of sand, not on the hard realities of life.

As hard as an individual may try, making wise decisions in life are not always a certainty. The downside of these decisions is that people often end up living a life that was never intended. It is not likely that an investigator will come across an instance of corruption where the perpetrator takes the position that she did it for the benefit of the people and not for her own enrichment.

Despite claims of outside influences, it is usually the case that the decision to engage in corruption is made by the corrupt individual seeking self-indulgence or an economic benefit. In some situations, an individual might feel the need to make financial ends meet or to respond to peer pressure, resentment, jealousy, revenge, or rage. These personal circumstances speak to the ego, the lack of integrity, and the lack of honesty of the individual perpetrating the fraud. It does not support any bogus idea of "the devil made me do it."

There is also an unfortunate truth that some people are just evil and intent on doing evil things. As Edmund Burke so famously stated, "All that is necessary for evil to triumph is that good men do nothing." Let us be good men doing something.

The PHA manager was sentenced to 4 years and 2 months in federal prison. She was also ordered to repay PHA $25,000 and to be on supervised probation for 3 years after her release.[11] In the scheme she hatched with corrupt contractors, they agreed that they would ultimately pay her $25,000 in bribes. The contractors would then pass the expense for the bribes onto the PHA by charging higher prices for work done. According to the indictment against the manager, PHA paid $283,756 for services that included the kickbacks. The work actually done was only worth $199,989.[12]

---

11 Ibid.

12 Ibid.

It is just an illusion

In another PHA bid-rigging scheme, a contractor admitted that his company existed solely on paper. The bogus company had no real business location and none of the typical equipment expected to be seen in a contracting business. Despite the fact that the company only existed on paper, it was able to receive hundreds of thousands of dollars in contracts from the PHA. This was while the purported owner of the company and lone employee was living in Phoenix, Arizona.

The sham business only existed on the stationery it used to submit proposals to PHA as part of the bid-rigging scheme that involved contractors who also paid bribes to PHA staff. The scheme resulted in the PHA paying inflated prices on these contracts.

The success of the scheme relied on the bogus company performing the required work on winning contracts through another company that was purporting to be a competing bidder for the work. When the company won a contract, the company falsely posing as the competing contractor did the work and forwarded a percentage of the contract amount to the company that only existed on paper.

No-competition-bid schemes

Not all bid-rigging schemes are solely between competing companies. Unfortunately, many schemes are formed between an individual company and procurement officer. Some of the more common schemes of this type are telephone-bid schemes. Telephone-bid schemes are also known as *loose lips* and *phantom bid* schemes, which are two of the most active between procurement officers and contractors.

Loose-lips scheme. These schemes only require an agreement between a single contractor and a procurement official. These schemes are the easiest to detect of the bid-rigging schemes. Loose lips occur in low-dollar procurements, usually $10,000 or less. In many jurisdictions, these types of procurements require the procurement official to contact three potential bidders over the phone and obtain a bid amount once the procurement official describes the commodities needed.

When rigging the bid, the procurement official already has an agreement in place with the contractor to contact him last. On that last call, the procurement official will advise the coconspirator what bids the previous two bidders made and then ask for the conspirator's bid. If the conspiring contractor wants to win the bid, he offers a bid price slightly lower than the individual that had the low bid before making the conspiring call.

Phantom bids. Phantom bid schemes are similar to the loose-lips scheme except that the procurement official is more daring in his actions. In this case, the procurement official only makes one phone call, and that is to the contractor who is already a participant in the scheme. As for the other two bids, the procurement official will not make those calls. Instead, he will enter a bid amount of his choosing and falsely record on the bid documents that the bids were made by legitimate contractors.

This is an easy scheme to detect as long as OAC implements a routine policy of conducting random reviews of the bidding process. Make a habit of calling one or more of the companies listed on the bidding documents, and confirm that the company, in fact, did submit the recorded bid amount. Each call will not reveal provable bid-rigging. However, it is statistically likely that a persistent strategy of making these calls will uncover bid-rigging schemes of the phantom-bid type.

In a phantom bid-rigging, scheme, a Bensalem school facilities manager and eight contractors were charged with offenses that included criminal conspiracy, bribery, and bid-rigging and tampering with public records. The evidence determined that on multiple occasions, the facilities manager compromised the bidding process by ensuring that contracts went to contractors involved in his bid-rigging scheme. In return, the manager received more than

$100,000 in cash, gifts, and construction work that was done on his home.

The Bensalem school district had an established policy that there are at least three bids for projects valued between $4,000 and $10,000. The facilities manager disregarded the policy and instead, working with contractors, made up a series of bogus bids to give the impression that he was following the established policy and that the competitive bidding process was in play.[13]

Political-influence schemes

Another area that has kept investigators and prosecutors active is the rigging of bids by politicians and members of their staffs or consulting concerns. In most instances of politicians rigging bids, it is done by flexing their political muscle and/or calling in favors.

An example of bid-rigging involving Pennsylvania politicians, contractors, procurement officials, and consultants relate to the bid-rigging schemes uncovered during the

13 "Ex-Bensalem School Official and 8 Contractors to Stand Trial Bid-rigging is suspected" http://articles.philly.com/1995-06-10/news/25691286_1_bid rigging-contractors-district-justice (accessed June 28, 2014).

course of the Pennsylvania Turnpike construction project. A grand jury formed to investigate allegations of corruption on the project issued an eighty-five-page report documenting political favoritism, bid-rigging, kickbacks, and influence peddling at the Turnpike Commission. When the project began in October of 2004, it had a projected cost of $181 million dollars. When it was completed in December 2008, it had a final cost of $330 million dollars—an 82 percent increase from the projected cost.[14]

The grand jury report outlined that top Turnpike officials solicited contractors for campaign contributions to favored politicians and took gifts of international travel, sports events, and lavish meals. In return, the contributors' companies received multimillion-dollar contracts, even when other bidders were less expensive and more qualified.

The following is the opening statement from the grand-jury report detailing the investigative findings and the individuals found to have engaged in what seemed to be an endless list of frauds against the people:

---

14 "New details emerge on FBI raid at Pennsylvania Turnpike," http://tollroadsnews.com/news/new-details-emerge-on-fbi-raid-at-pennsylvania-turnpike—second-source-confirms (accessed October 3, 2014).Thank you! Share Grammarly on Facebook!

INTRODUCTION

We, the members of the 33rd Statewide Investigating Grand Jury, having received and reviewed evidence regarding allegations of violations of the Pennsylvania Crime Code and related laws, occurring in Dauphin County, Pennsylvania, pursuant to notice of submission of Investigation No. 21, do hereby make the following findings of fact, conclusions, and recommendation of charges.

FINDINGS OF FACT

This investigation was commenced and continued as the result of public allegations of potential public corruption and criminal misconduct within the Pennsylvania Turnpike Commission ("the Turnpike" or "PTC" or "the Commission"). The Grand Jury investigation was initially commenced before the 31st Statewide Investigating Grand Jury in May of 2009, and, upon expiration of that Grand Jury, this matter was transferred to the attention of the 33rd Statewide Investigating Grand Jury in June of 2011. The 33rd Statewide Investigating Grand Jury issues this Presentment in furtherance of its ongoing investigation of the Pennsylvania Turnpike Commission.

In particular both the 31st and 33rd Statewide Investigating Grand Juries heard testimony from hundreds of witnesses; reviewed a wide range of exhibits, to include correspondence, emails, campaign contribution records, photographs, audio recordings, contracts, invoices, bank records, phone records, internal Turnpike policies and memoranda, expense reports, among other items; and considered and investigated referrals from the Turnpike's Office of Inspector General. The investigation before the respective Grand Juries, to date, has spanned forty-four months. Through its expansive and thorough inquiry, the 33rd Statewide Investigating Grand Jury ("the Grand Jury") has identified significant criminal wrongdoing on the part of Turnpike officials and vendors, and state legislators concerning the Turnpike's contracting and employment practices.

The Grand Jury has identified the following persons as having criminal responsibility and intent in the implementation, maintenance, and exercise of their authority over the Turnpike.

Robert Mellow was elected to the State Senate in 1970 and was the Democratic Caucus leader from 1989 through 2010. Mellow represented the 22nd district, which included all of Lackawanna County, and neighboring portions of Monroe and Luzerne Counties. When the Democrats held the majority in the Senate from 1992 to 1994, Mellow served as the President Pro Tempore. Mellow also served as the Democratic Floor Leader until his retirement in 2010.

Anthony Lepore served as his Chief of Staff during a significant portion of his tenure in Senate Leadership. As an elected official, Mellow was bound by the requirements of the State Ethics Act. Despite that fact, the Grand Jury finds that Mellow was actively involved in steering Turnpike contracts to particular vendors, imposing fundraising participation on Turnpike executive staff and Turnpike vendors, and personally benefiting from sports entertainment paid for by a significant vendor with the Turnpike.

Mitchell Rubin is a former chairman of the Pennsylvania Turnpike Commission. In 1998 and through the influence of Senator #6, Rubin was named to the Turnpike Commission. In 2003, Rubin was elected Chairman of the Turnpike Commission until his removal by the Governor in 2009. As a Commissioner with the Turnpike, Rubin was bound by the requirements of the State Ethics Act. Senator #6 exerted great influence over Rubin and, as a direct result, Rubin influenced contracting decisions made by executive staff at the Turnpike and regularly advocated that campaign contributions be made by Turnpike vendors to Senator #6 and other state officials. In addition, Rubin personally benefitted financially from Turnpike work he steered to City Line Abstract Company.

Joseph Brimmeier is the former Chief Executive Officer ("CEO") of the Pennsylvania Turnpike Commission. Brimmeier was a campaign confidant for Gubernatorial

Candidate #1. Following the successful campaign, the Governor appointed Brimmeier CEO of the Turnpike on February 4, 2003. As Chief Executive Officer of the Turnpike, Brimmeier was bound by the requirements of the State Ethics Act. Numerous witnesses testifying before the Grand Jury described Brimmeier as heavy-handed and extremely involved in all major decisions at the Turnpike. In addition, Brimmeier quickly aligned himself with the Senate Democrats and took orders directly from Senator Mellow, or his Chief of Staff Anthony Lepore, concerning the awarding of Turnpike contracts to particular vendors, and political fundraising efforts required of Turnpike personnel and Turnpike vendors.

George Hatalowich is the former Chief Operating Officer ("COO") and former Contracts Administrator of the Pennsylvania Turnpike Commission. Both positions bound Hatalowich by the requirements of the State Ethics Act. Hatalowich took direction from Turnpike Chairman Rubin and Turnpike CEO Brimmeier, and exerted tremendous influence over the internal processes at the Turnpike, resulting in the award of Turnpike contracts to those vendors favored by certain Senate officials. Hatalowich was also extremely active in the political fundraising activities, in particular by soliciting campaign contributions from Turnpike vendors which benefited Senators and Gubernatorial Candidates alike.

Dennis Miller is currently employed by Ciber as their Vice President of State and Local Government and Education for the United States, and also served there in a sales and marketing position. He was intrinsically involved in securing for Ciber approximately $82 million in Turnpike contracts by using his relationship with the Turnpike's Chief Information Officer ("CIO") to secure the work and improperly influence the contracting process. Further, Miller actively duplicated and created unnecessary work billed to the Turnpike, thereby significantly increasing his bonus payments and profit sharing with Ciber. Miller also developed a close relationship with Hatalowich and often bragged of his relationship to Rubin and political fundraising efforts for Senator #6.

Jeffrey Suzenski is the owner of Commonwealth Consulting Services, Inc. and a partial owner of Twin County Construction. Commonwealth Consulting Services represents TransCore and Twin County Construction, Inc., both long-term vendors with the Pennsylvania Turnpike Commission. Suzenski lavishly entertained Hatalowich, Rubin, and others at the expense of his clients, TransCore and Twin County Construction, in an effort to influence the awarding of Turnpike work to both entities, as well as to directly benefit himself.

The Grand Jury finds a prima facie case that these individuals, both individually and in concert with one another, committed and attempted to commit a series of crimes, including illegal bid-rigging, commercial bribery, conflict of interest, theft by unlawful taking, theft by deception, criminal conspiracy, and acted as a corrupt organization. Their criminal acts resulted in the misdirection, misuse, and theft of substantial amounts of public monies. Moreover, these individuals, employed by or associated with the Pennsylvania Turnpike Commission, used the Turnpike as an enterprise through which they engaged in commerce and, in the conduct of the Turnpike's affairs, a pattern of racketeering activity. These individuals wielded extraordinary power which they wrongfully used for self-enrichment and for their own political purposes, rather than for the good of the Commonwealth and its citizens.

Am I My Brother's Keeper?

The trouble with most of us is that
we would rather be ruined by praise
than saved by criticism.

—Norman Vincent Peale

OVER THE YEARS, corruption has adorned itself in many disguises. Most often, it has cloaked itself, not as just a purported friend, but a friend with something to offer at a time of need, such as a contractor with the resources needed to help meet the agency mission.

It has been said, "Beware of false prophets, who come to you in sheep's clothing, but inwardly they are ravening wolves. You shall know them by their fruits."[1] The verse is essentially saying, "Check out the people that you do business with before entering into any agreements. They will all herald grand benefits from the relationship and in the end

---

1 Matthew 7:15 "Watch out for false prophets. They come to you." *Biblehub.com*, http://biblehub.com/matthew/7-15.htm (accessed July 7, 2014).

will gladly try to convince you to buy wooden legs for your termite inspectors."

Throughout this discussion, the common idea stressed has been controlling the procurement process. Control is the goal. It is through the due-diligence process where control is initially established. How an organization goes about conducting its due-diligence and integrity checks to ensure it is about to collaborate with reputable individuals and organizations is an extremely significant process. In fact, it is in this process where the standard is set with respect to what is acceptable to the PHA and more importantly, what is not acceptable. Here is where the bar is set that contractors must attain. Here is where an organization establishes its in-house insurance policy against fraud.

Corruption fighters must recognize that corruption can have disastrous effects on an organization. A policy of being proactive in the fight will unmask individuals disguised as organizations of good character and high integrity. An aggressive, unyielding commitment by the OAC will consistently result in victory after victory in the cause.

A thorough and fair background check can be the cornerstone in uncovering frauds such as bid-rigging. These checks are an investment against unscrupulous contractors infiltrating the procurement process. The prudent course of action in combating fraud would be to establish a policy requiring that contractors be put through an integrity check—in essence, an ethics review—before allowing them to do business with the PHA.

There are a number of methods available to safeguard governmental systems that, if properly implemented, would make it difficult for corruption to gain a stronghold in the PHA. Taking a thorough look at the contractor's past can help in determining if it is in the best interest of the PHA to engage the contractor's services in the future.

Think about it. PHA employees who elect to engage in corruption will rely upon unscrupulous contractors to pay bribes for the services provided by these officials in executing corruption schemes. A thorough due-diligence program in many instances will prevent businesses with integrity and ethics issues from obtaining PHA contracts. This, in turn, eliminates the source of funding for the PHA employee seeking to engage in criminal enterprises, such as bid-rigging, with corrupt contractors.

Like Thieves in the Night

Few companies are 100 percent honest. Investigators must recognize that once specifications have been written and a contract advertised for bidding, proper prescreening and due diligence are the next lines of defense in warding off deceitful individuals attempting to infiltrate the PHA's noble efforts to serve the people. Without prescreening and due diligence, organizations of questionable integrity will creep into the PHA like thieves in the night and undermine the valuable work being done on behalf of the people of Philadelphia.

Integrity reviews are synonymous with being proactive. A significant part of what OAC is called upon to do is to be proactive in its thinking and actions. Prescreening and due diligence through the utilization of various information databases available are an absolute must if OAC is serious about taking the fight to the doorsteps of the bad guys.

An integrity review should begin with a background check of the principals, company name, and a list of other projects, both private and public, performed by the contractor. There are a number of public and nonpublic databases available to assist in confirming the good character of an organization or individual seeking to do business with the PHA. Take the time to determine the subsidiaries and affiliates of the bidders for a contract. The review should include a close look at addresses, post-office boxes, and vehicle registrations.

The following are just some of the databases and resources available to investigators when conducting integrity checks:

Credit checks. Information concerning a company's financial ability to perform on a contract is extremely valuable. Companies will often misrepresent this ability. In fact, financial woes can be an excuse offered by contractors for engaging in bid-rigging schemes. Credit checks can be done by accessing databases provided by such organizations as Transunion, Equifax, and Experian. Additional information about a company can be determined through organizations such as Dun and Bradstreet, Westlaw, LexisNexis, and TLO. These databases and ones similar to these are an invaluable tool in determining current and past principals, affiliates, company name variations, judgments and liens, addresses, and motor vehicles, as well as relatives and associates.

Do not treat databases as infallible tools of technology. Keep in mind that while the information uncovered is usually relevant with respect to the company, there are times that the information is not up to date. Do not discount the importance and value of taking the time to speak to people who might have knowledge about the area, company, or individual being check.

Articles of incorporation (AI). You will find that companies do not always reveal the names of all of their principals for background purposes. AIs are an excellent source of information in determining the principals of companies. AIs are also referred to as a certificate of incorporation or the corporate charter. They are usually filed with a state or other regulatory agency.

State division of corporations. State divisions of corporations, in addition to providing information on principals of companies, can also alert you to tax warrants on the company as well as its principals.

State attorney general databases. These databases can alert you to criminal and civil matters involving the company, both past and present.

Criminal history checks. If there is no method in place for checking the criminal history of a contractor, then the integrity review is not complete. This is where an investigator will have the greatest success in detecting individuals of questionable character attempting to infiltrate the system. There should be a policy requiring a contractor to explain any arrest or conviction and document the disposition.

Google, MSN, or other Internet checks. There is a wealth of information concerning contractors and principals within various Internet databases. Dig beyond the first few screens; often that is where you may find negative information concerning a contractor. Do not limit your searches to your jurisdiction. Corruption has gone global; any integrity review undertaken must do the same.

System for Award Management (SAM). This is the United States General Services Administration's database. The SAM is a public database that provides information on federal contractors and persons who have negative information involving past performance on federal contracts or who are prohibited from being awarded federal contracts. In many instances, these organizations do not limit their activities to the federal level. It is likely that they are also contracting on state and local levels as well. There are also various databases maintained by individual states listing companies that are banned from doing business with those states.

Department of Justice (DOJ) database. The DOJ database can be a source of negative information that the DOJ may have on a contractor.

Department of Treasury specially designated nationals (SDN) list. As part of its enforcement efforts, Treasury publishes a list of individuals and companies owned or controlled by, or acting for or on behalf of, targeted countries. It also lists individuals, groups, and entities, such as terrorists and narcotics traffickers, designated under programs that are not country-specific. Collectively, such individuals and companies are called specially designated nationals, or SDNs. Their assets are blocked, and US persons are generally prohibited from dealing with them. Checking the SDN should be a routine step in any integrity review.

Press releases. An integrity review should always include a review of press releases issued by prosecutors, other law-enforcement agencies, and the company itself that is being reviewed. Media are a great source of information on organizations with questionable character. Take the time to search press releases, as well as databases that keep track of negative news articles, to determine if derogatory news is available on the organization you are about to do business with.

Once these checks have been conducted, steps should be taken to determine if there is a relationship between any of the companies bidding or actually working on a project. Your integrity check should take steps to determine the following:

- Do any vendors on the project have a business relationship?
- Does that relationship involve an ownership interest in either of the businesses?
- Did principals properly report the existence of this relationship?
- Do vendors have a financial relationship, such as shared bank accounts, equipment, or property?
- When did the relationship begin?

- Does this relationship exist on any nongovernment projects?
- Was a corporation established for purposes of this business relationship?
- Are there family relationships that exist within this business relationship?
- Do the principals in the relationship have the required verifiable experience?

Once this has all been verified, these additional steps should be taken.

- Prioritize the issues that have arisen that are a cause for concern.
- Determine whether issues will have an immediate impact on the project.
- Do issues relate to the company, principals, or both?
- Do issues relate to vendor integrity or general responsibility?
- Are issues of a criminal nature?
- Do issues relate to current or past matters concerning the vendor or principals?
- Are law enforcement agencies or prosecutors investigating issues?
- What additional records need to be obtained?
- What interviews need to be done?

- Who should make up the investigative team?
- Determine how much time you have to resolve these issues before they have a negative impact on PHA.
- Who, if anyone, needs to be notified that these issues exist?

Integrity review is not a process that should be seen as routine. Most contractors engaging in bid-rigging schemes will be found to have engaged in questionable behavior in the past. There is an absolute need for a corruption-fighting entity to be proactive in its approach to the fight. If the plan is to wait for a complaint before opening an investigation, the coffers will already have been raided by the time the investigation begins.

The Bid-Rigging Checklist

If a man is called to be a street sweeper, he should sweep streets even as Michelangelo painted or Beethoven composed music or Shakespeare wrote poetry. He should sweep streets so well that all the host of heaven and earth will pause to say, "Here lived a great street sweeper who did his job well."

—Dr. Martin Luther King Jr

It is understood that bid-rigging is a complicated scheme and difficult to substantiate. Without the cooperation of someone with specific knowledge of the conspiracy, it will require a review of bids, bid tabulation sheets, and bidding activity over a period of time, most likely three to five years, depending on the number of contractors and bidders being reviewed. It is unlikely, but not impossible, that the review and analysis of one contract will uncover provable bid-rigging.

There are a number of ways to detect bid-rigging. The initial step in the investigative process should be to prepare a bid-rigging checklist to be used by procurement staff when reviewing bid submissions and by investigative staff when considering investigations.

The checklist will be the foundation for the construction of a bid-rigging matrix. The matrix is a spreadsheet detailing bidding activity by several contractors over a period of time. These two documents will be extremely valuable in helping an investigator analyze the bid-rigging indicators. They also have the potential to be significant pieces of evidence when prosecuting the case. The checklist should include, but not be limited to, the following questions:

- ☐ Have a review of bid-tabulation sheets and other documents uncovered instances of companies submitting bids higher than established price list?
- ☐ Have any company's submitted bids higher than bids previously submitted by the company for the same service or commodity?
- ☐ Are bids significantly higher than estimates without reasonable explanations?
- ☐ Are there instances of inconsistent and unexplained price increases?
- ☐ Is there a pattern of a group consisting of companies taking turns at being the successful bidder?
- ☐ Are there instances of one or more companies repeatedly submitting unsuccessful bids?

- ☐ Are there instances where the winning bidder frequently subcontracts work to failed bidders?
- ☐ Have there been companies withdrawing successful bids for no ostensible reason and later awarded subcontracting work by the winning contractor?
- ☐ Do instances exist where different submissions have identical areas not filled out?
- ☐ Are there instances of prices remaining identical for long periods?
- ☐ Are there instances of bid submissions with identical bid amounts, either by line item or in total?
- ☐ Are there identical errors in calculations, spelling, similar handwriting, typeface, or stationery in the bids submitted by different contractors?
- ☐ Are there cases of companies submitting bids that do not have the appropriate resources or the skill set to complete the project?
- ☐ Do bid or price documents contain whiteouts or other alterations indicating last-minute changes?
- ☐ Do bid prices decrease when a new bidder enters the competition?
- ☐ Do contractors obtain bid packages for themselves and other companies?
- ☐ Do contractors submit bids for themselves and other contractors?

- ☐ Has procurement staff observed companies bringing more than one bid to an opening, and that company submits a bid after seeing who else is bidding?
- ☐ Are the same companies winning a specific type of procurement?
- ☐ Has the analysis revealed inconsistent pricing in bids by certain companies with no apparent cost differences to account for the inconsistency?
- ☐ Are there instances where bids are postmarked from the same location but the contractor's place of business is not located in the area of the postmark?
- ☐ Are there instances of the same notary public being used by multiple bidders?
- ☐ Are there instances of too many or too few bids submitted?
- ☐ Are there large gaps between the winning bid and the remaining submissions?
- ☐ Are there proper controls in place for receipt of bids?
- ☐ Have principals or company representatives made statements of concern such as:
- ☐ knowledge of price schedules;
- ☐ knowledge of a competitors' pricing;
- ☐ complementary bids are being submitted.

Upon completing the checklist, review each answer for any indications of suspect behavior, no matter how minor.

Take the time to be deliberate and thorough in reviewing each answer. For each answer that appears to be suspect even in the slightest terms, include that information in the bid-rigging or competition matrix.

The Bid-Rigging Matrix

Try not to become a man of success
but rather try to become a man of value.

—*Albert Einstein*

Keep in mind that the information amassed in the course of preparing the bid-rigging checklist are only indicators of a possible bid-rigging scheme. Once a review of the data in the checklist is complete, the next step in the analysis should be to establish a competition matrix.

There is no set requirement as to how far back a competition matrix should go in this analysis. It makes the most sense to cover the period of the statute of limitations. In the state of Pennsylvania, that would be three years for fraud and eight years if the crime involves official misconduct.[1] The matrix would include, but not be limited to, the following:

1 "Pennsylvania Criminal Statute of Limitations" http://www.criminaldefenselawyer.com/criminal-case-statute-of-limitations/PA-felonies-misdemeanors.htm%26quot; (accessed June 29, 2014)

- List of major contractors competing on projects
- Number of contracts they were awarded during the matrix review period
- Dollar volume these contracts represented
- Percentage of the total contracts and the total dollar volume won by each vendor
- Ranking of the contractors based on the above[2]

When preparing the bid-rigging matrix, it is best to begin with a review of the bidding checklist, followed by an analysis of bid tabulation sheets. In the initial review, keep the matrix simple. Do not overload it with too much information. At this point in the process, the goal is to seek indicators of bid-rigging and to do this in a relatively short period. Expanding on the matrix is always an option at a later date.

When reviewing bids, it is important to note the qualifications of each of the bidders who participated in the bidding process. There will be instances where bid submissions will, in fact, be complementary bids where scheme participants do not possess the capacity or skill set to perform the project even though they submitted a bid

2 "Suggestions for Detection and Prevention of Construction Contract Bid Rigging" http://www.fhwa.dot.gov/program admin/contracts/dotjbid.cfm (accessed June 28, 2014).

suggesting that the company was capable of completing the contract.

In preparing to construct a bid-rigging matrix, be sensitive to those contracts that involved five or fewer bidders. Contracts that fall into this category should be considered for inclusion in the bid-rigging matrix. The matrix should include the following information:

1. A list of all prequalified bidders and their capabilities–this is important information. There are times that companies participating in bid rigging schemes will submit complementary bids knowing that the company is not capable of providing the service being requested.
2. Line-item prices on suspect jobs–pay close attention to line-item prices. When the total amount of a bid might be in line with estimates, line items are often inconsistent with market rates or suppler pricing. This can also be an indicator of a complementary bid.
3. Identity of all subcontractors on suspect jobs–in a large percentage of cases, participants in bid rigging schemes benefit through being given subcontracting assignments on the project where the bid is rigged.

4. A list of each company that received bid packages on the suspect jobs.
5. With respect to contracts requiring concrete or asphalt, the analysis should include a review of the location and capacity of each contractor's plants. This analysis will be helpful in uncovering geographic bid rigging schemes.
6. Has the bidding checklist and other analysis conducted determined that there are unusual instances of contractors repeatedly bidding against one another, or are there certain contractors who do not bid against one another?
7. Has the analysis painted a picture where successful bidders repeatedly subcontract work to companies that submitted higher bids on the same projects, or that picked up bid packages, but did not submit bids?
8. Are there instances of a particular contractor always winning in a certain geographical area? This can be an indicator of a geographic market allocation scheme being in place.
9. Are there instances of contractors who frequently bid but never win? If so, this suggests the strong possibility of complementary bidding being in place.
10. Has the checklist uncovered instances of identical bid amounts on a contract line item by two or more contractors? This may be an indicator of collusion

where one of the companies prepares the paperwork for co-conspirators.

11. Has any of the bidders been previously suspected or proven to be a participant in a bid-rigging scheme?
12. In instances of contracts being rebid, is there a failure of original bidders to rebid or an identical ranking of the same bidders upon rebidding, where original bids were rejected for being too far over the estimate?[3] Original bidders dropping out is a strong indication that honest competitors became aware of the bid-rigging scheme and dropped out of the competition or that they were approached by the schemers and encouraged to drop out. The identical ranking indicates that the companies involved in the scheme have already predetermined the outcome of the bidding.

Again, remember, this is not a process intended to produce solid evidence of Bid-rigging. It is a process intended to bring to light indicators that a scheme is afoot.

3 Ibid.

The Game Is Afoot

When evil men plot, good men must plan.
When evil men shout ugly words of hatred,
good men must commit themselves to the glories of love.

—Dr. Martin Luther King Jr.

As Sherlock Holmes so often stated to Dr. Watson, "The game is afoot."

Once the proper due diligence is completed, checklist reviewed, and matrix constructed, the indicators will roll out at your feet. It is here where it will truly be recognized that the game is, in fact, afoot. The indicators have been revealed; let the investigation begin!

There are several steps to take once the available information suggests that a bid-rigging investigation should be commenced. The opening volley in your course of action should be intended to reveal who is actually bidding on PHA projects. Remember, bid-rigging investigations take shape after investigative research; review of the bid-rigging checklist and preparation of the Bid-rigging matrix comes together and paints a picture over time of what is taking place.

Information on who is bidding is essential. Such information provides

- intelligence on who is bidding as it relates to location,
- who is bidding as it relates to frequency of bids,
- who is bidding as it relates to the bidding company's ability to complete the project,
- who is not bidding (many honest contractors will cease bidding when they become aware of the fact that a bid-rigging scheme is operational in the area).

Make an effort to find out who these contractors are and seek input from them. In addition, some participants in the scheme will not bid as part of the bid-rigging plan. It is a useful idea to bring those contractors in for an interview at some point and question them as to why they are not bidding.

It is also a useful idea to create a policy where any company on a PHA-established bidders list that fails to bid on more than three consecutive projects for which they are clearly qualified be reevaluated for continued participation on the list. In a number of instances, companies will seek inclusion on the bidder's list simply to be in a position to submit complementary bids when the need arises.

Once the initial step of determining who is bidding is underway, it would be useful to focus on who is doing the work. Bid-rigging investigations require investigators to get up from their desk, go into the field, and see what is actually taking place on construction sites, at warehouses, and other locations where procured product is delivered or in use.

Investigators must get out to the site and see which contractors are doing the work and how it relates to those who bid on the project. There will be instances where the winning bidder will award parts of the contract to competitors in return for submitting complementary bids or no bid at all.

While going through this process, take the time to identify the prime contractors and the principals of those companies. Check to see if any of the principals have a connection to any of the other companies that may have bid on the project. It is possible that companies with affiliates and companies operating under different names will bid against themselves.

It is advantageous to know who the reported subcontractors are. Once this has been determined, conduct an analysis to determine what role these companies may have played in the bidding process. They may have submitted complementary bids or taken some other measure to ensure the success of a rigged bid.

Most agencies that are adept at detecting various procurement-fraud schemes have rules in place that require an integrity review before a contractor or subcontractor is approved to operate on a project. PHA should be no different. It is also important to know who the actual, sometimes unreported, subcontractors are.

Pay attention to the companies actually on site doing the subcontractor work, not just those listed on the various reports submitted in the contract-management process. There can be times that a subcontractor actually doing the work is being paid back for not bidding or for submitting a complementary bid. There will also be times when unapproved contractors will be found on site. This is likely to be payback for a complementary bid.

It is just as important to know if any of these companies have relationships to each other, such as common owners. Knowing the principals of the subcontractors can alert an investigative team to any potential collusion as, for example, between common owners, relatives, or former business partners.

The bottom line is, do not disregard the research that needs to be done on these organizations. Determine who the players are and what relationships exist among them, both on the scene and behind the scenes. Knowing the above is necessary in order to know whether part of the profits was shared with a competitor.

All participants in bid-rigging conspiracies are in it for the money. A lucrative part of any contract is connected to the company providing the materials and equipment for the project. Often in bid-rigging schemes, there are agreements made with contractors not to bid, with the understanding that they will supply certain materials and equipment for the project.

Again, verify that the suppliers were not also bidders who may have submitted complementary bids or that the supplier was not a significant player in other bids submitted for the project. Also, take time to ensure that the supplier is not being paid for his complementary bid by providing inferior materials, expired product, or obsolete parts for his role in a subcontractor bid-rigging scheme.

When trying to determine if the bid-rigging scheme involves aspects of market allocation or some other geographic assignment of contracts as part of the conspiracy, it is advantageous to know the location of all bidders and nonbidders in relation to the job.

Make an effort to determine where the bidders and suppliers have their base of operation. Did all the potential bidders bid? Did the supplier originally bid as a prime contractor or a subcontractor?

Many conspiracies work toward ensuring that each conspirator gets the jobs closest to the conspirator's place of business, which reduces expenses, thereby raising profit.

An effort will always be made to try to make these schemes as lucrative for participants as possible. Another profitable aspect of contracts, especially construction contracts, rests in who is transporting project materials. This does not necessarily have to be the same company that is supplying the material. Trucking is a lucrative business. Many contractors include delivery of supplies through its trucking component of the business as a service. These companies will happily refrain from bidding, with the understanding that the winning bidder will give the trucking contract to a coconspirator who refrained from bidding or submitted a complementary bid.

Again, in detecting market-allocation schemes, it is necessary to know who wins what, where, and when. Understanding who wins the contract, where, and when, will alert investigators to geographic bid-rigging schemes and bid-rotation schemes.

As in all aspects of investigations, an investigator always wants to know why something is happening. Bid-rigging is no different. Any investigator with even basic skills will always want to know the reasons why things are happening. For every piece of information and intelligence obtained, ask the question, "Why?" If the whys do not make sense, this means that there are more rocks to overturn.

The process described above has proven invaluable in conducting bid-rigging investigations. They provide the background information that enables investigators to conduct the detailed interviews required to move the investigation in a successful direction. Successful prosecutions have resulted principally from the testimony of individuals who were involved in the schemes. This analysis can lead to those individuals.

Fighting Corruption Is Not a Spectator Sport

If, to please the people, we offer what we ourselves disapprove, how can we afterward defend our work? Let us raise a standard to which the wise and honest can repair.

—George Washington

Corruption-fighting organizations such as the OAC must be adept at identifying instances of fraud against the government, in particular, in the procurement process. Having said this, investigators must recognize that agencies such as the PHA cannot accomplish this task in isolation. Government and the law-enforcement agencies responsible for legislative action and investigative deterrence in combating fraud will need the support and assistance of all government employees. In this instance, it includes those involved in the procurement process. It is imperative that all of the players take all reasonable steps to detect and eliminate fraud, waste, and abuse. In the case of the PHA, it begins with OAC establishing itself as the preverbal immovable force defying those who dare challenge its resolve.

Fighting corruption is a team effort; there is no sideline, dugout, or bench. Investigators and procurement staff alike must join the fight from kickoff to the final whistle. All PHA staff, contractors, and tenants should be encouraged to report suspicions of collusion to the OAC. Once this is done, do not make promises to cooperators that every reported suspicion will result in an investigation. However, do not hesitate to give assurances that every report is taken seriously and will be carefully considered and given the appropriate scrutiny.

Explain to complainants that their observations may add to the information already under review, which, together with other reports, may indicate a more widespread problem. Advise them that their call will always be appreciated and treated in accordance with OAC's confidentiality policy.

Respect the process

PHA relies upon open, arm's length, and competitive procurements to assure that it expends the public's resources wisely. The authority should only do business with contractors who will respect the procurement process and will adhere to its various guidelines.

Contractors are expected to behave honestly and in accordance with the terms of their contracts and PHA's code of conduct. Establishing and maintaining a productive relationship with the PHA entails an understanding of the authority's needs, requirements, and ethical environment.

Unfortunately, there will be those who seek an advantage by utilizing unethical or illegal methods. If the authority's interests are to be protected, fraud and illegal activity must be addressed by a combination of criminal, civil, regulatory, and contractual remedies. That leaves the OAC with the chore of being prepared to defend against fraud and utilize the appropriate remedies to bring violators to justice. Achieving this goal depends upon the sound judgment and alertness of OAC staff responsible for ensuring the integrity of the procurement process, from specification to delivery.

Carpe Diem!

It is not the critic who counts; not the man who points out how the strong man stumbles, or where the doer of deeds could have done them better. The credit belongs to the man who is actually in the arena; whose face is marred by dust and sweat and blood; who strives valiantly; who errs and comes up short again and again; because there is no effort without error or shortcoming, but who knows the great enthusiasms, the great devotions, and spends himself in a worthy cause; who, at the best, knows, in the end, the triumph of high achievement; and who at worst, if he fails, at least fails while daring greatly, so that his place shall never be with those cold and timid souls who knew neither victory nor defeat."

—*Theodore Roosevelt*

In order to identify and eradicate corruption, corruption-fighting agencies must forcefully seize the day and go about drawing on the best practices of the present-day corruption-fighting agencies with all of the components available to ensure success. Each factor is critical in helping that agency accomplish its stated mission. Once the agency has been established and partners in successful investigations and prosecutions, the goal of ensuring the integrity of government operations and fostering economic fairness, and efficiencies will be well within reach.

While the ideas and methods discussed in these pages have been found to be effective in addressing bid-rigging, do not see them as a magic potion to eradicate the fraud. If you are serious about waging battle in this arena, you must accept the fact that corruption breeds some incredibly inventive people intent on subverting the system for personal benefit.

There will always be people who think they can beat the system and commit the perfect crime. The only way that they will be successful is if those of us chosen to stand in the gap become complacent, cocky, and arrogant about who we are and what we do.

It is imperative that we never allow the feeling of discouragement to enter into our hearts or minds; far too many of us plan for the positive but are intent on walking in the negative.

There is nothing easy about this profession. Remember, we are life changers. Do not take that lightly. What we do as professionals requires each of us to take a seat on the same emotional roller coaster that our subjects, witnesses, victims, and even families are riding. Experiencing success and failure are a part of that emotional ride. In many respects, the emotions you will experience will help to validate who you are as a combatant in this struggle and your wisdom in choosing to be a part of this noble profession. Nevertheless, there will be failures along the way. Those failures can be discouraging. Get over it!

The truth is that failures are not the only things that can discourage you in this business. A lack of appreciation for the work tends to take its toll on some of us at times. There will from time to time be a feeling that corrupt individuals are not adequately punished. Dealing with this requires a level of investigative maturity that comes with time.

Success in this mission will take you on an exceptionally complicated emotional path. Do not shy away from these situations or emotions while fighting corruption. No weapon formed against you shall prosper if you learn to reshape it for your use. Make it a part of your arsenal. Learn to embrace the emotion; it will unquestionably make you better at what you do.

No matter how adept you are today in deterring corruption, you must be better at it tomorrow. Corruption does not stand still; it moves and adjusts to the conditions and circumstances presented to it. You must do the same. There is a saying that "very often we find that those standing still are in reality moving further away from us all." In this fight, you cannot afford to stand still.

It is all about the seed

I would like you to take a moment and think about what it is that you are holding in your hands or looking at on your screen at this moment. It is not just a book, not just a collection of electronic data, not just a collection of words, ideas, and thoughts. What you have before you is a seed. Now you can take this seed and display it on a shelf in your office or library as if it were a collectible of some sort, save it on your computer or e-reader, or you can do with it what is meant to be done with a seed—plant it. Plant this seed by taking these ideas and sharing them with others who are also a part of the fight. Beyond that, I want you to take the seed and help to make it grow. Improve upon it; make it better than anything that I ever envisioned.

> To everything there is a season, and a time to every purpose under the heaven: A time to be born, and a time to die; a time to plant, and a time to pluck up that which is planted; A time to kill, and a time to heal; a time to break down, and a time to build up; A time to weep, and a time to laugh; a time to mourn, and a time to dance. (Eccles. 3:1–4, KJV)

My friends, the season of corruption must end. It serves no purpose in our nations, cities, communities, jobs, or families. It has lived a long life, and its death is long overdue. It is time to pluck up the tares of greed that have been planted on behalf of corruption. We must eradicate the idea and begin to heal the land. We must break down its stronghold wherever it exists and begin to plant fields of integrity, surrounded by walls of honor. The time for weeping and mourning is over. The joyous time for the parade of integrity to march through the necropolis of corruption has come.

It is now time for the fertile organizations of truth to plant the seeds of honor and integrity. It has been said that every seed produces after its kind. We know that corruption has planted seeds that reaped a harvest of more corruption. Integrity shall now plant deep-rooted seeds and reap a bountiful harvest of its kind.

Never forget that you have to have an expectation for your seed. Once planted, stop thinking about the seed and begin thinking about the harvest. Remember, the ground upon which you plant is as valuable as the seed. We must protect the ground in which we plant the seed. We must protect the people in anticipation of the harvest. You are the first produce of the seed planted, as such; you must be the light that illuminates the path of hope.

Let's go out and fight for it!

Early in my career, I developed a passion for this cause. I begin each day thanking the Lord for the blessing of being a warrior in this struggle, and I ask for strength and wisdom to continue the fight and to leave my mark on the cause.

Some years ago, I heard motivational speaker Les Brown end one of his presentations with the following words, which I begin each day with as my call to arms in this fight:

> If you want something bad enough, go out and fight for it. Work day and night for it.
> Give up your time, your peace and your sleep for it if all that you dream and scheme is about it, and life seems useless and worthless without it...
> if you'll gladly sweat for it, fret for it, plan for it, and lose all terror of the opposition for it...

if you simply go after that thing that you want with all your capacity, strength and sagacity, faith, hope, and confidence and stern pertinacity …
if neither cold, poverty, famine or gout, sickness nor pain of body or brain can keep you away from that thing that you want…
if dogged and grim you besiege and beset it. With the help of God, you will get it!

Carpe diem!

Bibliography

Fitzpatrick, Diana. *Criminal Defense Lawyer.com.* 2014. http://www.criminaldefenselawyer.com/criminal-case-statute-of-limitations/PA-felonies-misdemeanors.htm%26quot; (accessed July 1, 2014).

Jeremiah, Kelvin A. *Anti-Corruption Guide for PHA's Contractors and Vendors.* 12 2011. http://www.pha.phila.gov/media/80911/anti-corruption_guide_final_no_bleeds_1_25_12_web.pdf (accessed June 28, 2014).

Joseph Welsch. *U.S. Department of Transportation Federal Highway Administration.* February 1983. http://www.fhwa.dot.gov/programadmin/contracts/dotjbid.cfm (accessed July 1, 2014).

Jr., Walter F. Roche. *Philly.com.* June 23, 1994. http://articles.philly.com/1994-06-23/news/25834440_1_bid-rigging-home-detention-restitution (accessed July 1, 2014).

Jury, Pennsylvania 33rd Statewide Investigating Grand. *Pennsylvania Turnpike Grand Jury Presentation.* Grand

Jury Report, Dauphin County: Pennsylvania 33rd Statewide Grand Jury, 2013.

May, Don. *Bribery in the Construction Industry: Part II-Bid Rigging.* January 31, 2013. http://enewsletters.constructionexec.com/managingyourbusiness/2013/01/bribery-in-the-construction-industry-part-ii-bid-rigging/ (accessed June 28, 2014).

Purdy, Matthew. *philly.com.* June 22, 1993. http://articles.philly.com/1993-06-22/news/25972010_1_pha-contractors-scheme (accessed June 30, 2014).

Richard Berkowitz. *philly.com.* June 10, 1995. http://articles.philly.com/1995-06-10/news/25691286_1_bid-rigging-contractors-district-justice (accessed June 28, 2014).

Rosenberg, Amy S. *Philly.com.* March 31, 1995. http://articles.philly.com/1995-03-31/news/25699813_1_pha-inspections-extortion (accessed June 30, 2014).

Shah, Anup. *Global Issues.* September 24, 2011. http://www.globalissues.org/article/715/today-21000-children-died-around-the-world (accessed June 28, 2014).

Solobodzian, Joseph A. *Philly.com.* September 8, 1995. http://articles.philly.com/1995-09-08/news/25716320_1_pha-bribes-count-of-mail-fraud (accessed June 30, 2014).

Susan Caba. *philly.com.* September 30, 1993. http://articles.philly.com/1993-09-30/news/25986508_1_house-arrest-pha-housing-agency (accessed June 28, 2014).

INDEX

Photo, Courtesy of Sharinda Welton, The University of Findlay